Contents

2010/11

1) What was the result of the series?

2) Name the venue for each of the five tests

3) What was the result of each test?

4) From their initials, name every player who made an appearance for Australia during the series
M.B
D.B
M.C
X.D
B.H
R.H
B.H
P.H
M.H
M.J
S.K
U.K
M.N
R.P
P.S
S.S
S.W

5) From their initials, name every player who made an appearance for England during the series

J.A

I.B

T.B

S.B

P.C

A.C

S.F

K.P

M.P

A.S

G.S

C.T

J.T

6) Who were the head coaches of each side?

7) Who were the captains of each side?

8) Name the top 3 run scorers for Australia in the series

9) Name the top 3 run scorers for England in the series

10) Name the top 3 wicket-takers for Australia in the series

11) Name the top 3 wicket-takers for England in the series

12) Who won the man of the series award?

13) Which two Australians scored centuries in the series?

14) Which six Englishmen scored centuries in the series?

15) What was the highest partnership for each side in the series?

16) What was the highest total for each team in the series?

17) What was the lowest score each team was bowled out for in the series?

18) Who recorded the best match bowling figures for each sides?

19) Who scored the highest individual score for each side?

20) Name the three players who bowled in the series, but failed to take a wicket

21) Other than wicketkeepers, who took the most catches in the series?

22) Which four players were run-out in the series?

23) Which players were out stumped during the series?

24) How many wickets did Australia lose in the series?

25) How many wickets did England lose in the series?

26) Which five batsmen were dismissed for golden ducks during the series?

27) Which two players were dismissed for pairs during the series?

28) Which now common-place system was used in the Ashes for the first time in this series?

29) Who took a hat-trick on his birthday, during the first test?

30) Xaiver Doherty dismissed who to claim his first test wicket during the first test?

31) Andrew Strauss narrowly avoided a pair when he was struck on the pads leaving the first ball of the second innings. Who was the bowler?

32) What did England declare on in the 2nd innings of the first test?

33) Who dismissed Michael Clarke with the last ball of the fourth day of the second test to help push England towards victory?

34) Simon Katich was run-out in the 1st over of the second test without facing a ball, which England fielder threw down the stumps?

35) Who did James Anderson dismiss in the 2nd innings of the third test for his 200th test wicket?

36) Which future England one-day captain appeared as a substitute fielder during the series?

37) Who did England drop for the fourth test, despite him being the leading wicket-taker in the series at that point?

38) Who was the last man out for Australia when England retained the Ashes during the fourth test?

39) Who did Paul Collingwood's dismiss for his final ever test wicket in the 1st innings of the fifth test?

40) During the fifth test Alastair Cook became the second youngest player to reach 5000 runs, who was the only player younger than him to achieve this landmark?

41) Michael Beer was denied his first test match wicket for what reason when Alastair Cook was caught on 47 during the fifth test?

42) Michael Beer was again denied his first test match wicket when the Australians appealed for a catch when Cook was on 99, for what reason was the wicket not given?

43) Michael Beer finally claimed his first test wicket, and in doing so dismissed which England player who was playing his final ever test match?

44) Who was the not out batsman in the fifth test as England bowled Australia out to clinch the series?

2013

1) What was the result of the series?

2) Name the venue for each of the five tests

3) What was the result of each test?

4) From their initials, name every player who made an appearance for Australia during the series
   A.A
   J.B
   M.C
   E.C
   J.F
   B.H
   R.H
   P.H
   U.K
   N.L
   J.P
   C.R
   P.S
   S.S
   M.S
   D.W
   S.W

5) From their initials, name every player who made an appearance for England during the series
   J.A
   J.B
   I.B
   T.M
   S.B
   A.A
   S.F
   S.K
   K.P
   M.P
   J.R
   G.S
   J.T
   C.W

6) Who were the head coaches of each side?

7) Who were the captains of each side?

8) Name the top 3 run scorers for Australia in the series

9) Name the top 3 run scorers for England in the series

10) Name the top 3 wicket-takers for Australia in the series

11) Name the top 3 wicket-takers for England in the series

12) Who won the man of the series award?

13) Which four Australians scored centuries in the series?

14) Which three Englishmen scored centuries in the series?

15) What was the highest partnership for each side in the series?

16) What was the highest total for each team in the series?

17) What was the lowest score each team was bowled out for in the series?

18) Who recorded the best match bowling figures for each side?

19) Who scored the highest individual score for each side?

20) Name the two players who bowled in the series, but failed to take a wicket

21) Other than wicketkeepers, who took the most catches in the series?

22) Which players were run-out in the series?

23) How many players were out stumped during the series?

24) How many wickets did Australia lose in the series?

25) How many wickets did England lose in the series?

26) Which five batsmen were dismissed for golden ducks during the series?

27) How many players were dismissed for pairs during the series?

28) Who was sacked as Australia's coach just before the start of the series?

29) David Warner was serving a ban up until the first test after punching who in bar earlier in the summer?

30) James Pattinson bowled the first ball of the series, what happened?

31) How many runs did Philip Hughes and Ashton Agar add for the 10th wicket in the 1st innings of the first test?

32) Ashton Agar made what score batting at number 11 in his first ever test innings?

33) Stuart Broad infamously refused to walk and was given not-out after edging to first slip off the bowling of which Australian in the 2nd innings of the first test?

34) Which Australian hit his maiden test match hundred during the 4th test?

35) Steve Smith secured his first test match century by hitting which bowler for 6 during the fifth test?

36) Which two English bowlers made their test match debuts in the fifth test?

37) What happened to the first ball Chris Woakes faced in test cricket?

38) Chris Woakes had his first test wicket taken off him after which Australian successfully reviewed an LBW decision?

39) Which Australian all-rounder made his test match debut in the fifth test?

40) Brad Haddin claimed a world record by taking how many catches in the series?

2013/14

1) What was the result of the series?

2) Name the venue for each of the five tests

3) What was the result of each test?

4) From their initials, name every player who made an appearance for Australia during the series
G.B
M.C
B.H
R.H
M.J
N.L
C.R
P.S
S.S
D.W
S.W

5) From their initials, name every player who made an appearance for England during the series

J.A

J.B

G.B

I.B

S.B

T.B

S.B

M.C

A.C

S.F

M.P

K.P

M.P

B.R

J.R

B.S

G.S

C.T

J.T

6) Who were the head coaches of each side?

7) Who were the captains of each side?

8) Name the top 3 run scorers for Australia in the series

9) Name the top 3 run scorers for England in the series

10) Name the top 3 wicket-takers for Australia in the series

11) Name the top 3 wicket-takers for England in the series

12) Who won the man of the series award?

13) Which six Australians scored centuries in the series?

14) Which Englishman scored a century in the series?

15) What was the highest partnership for each side in the series?

16) What was the highest total for each team in the series?

17) What was the lowest score each team was bowled out for in the series?

18) Who recorded the best match bowling figures for each side?

19) Who scored the highest individual score for each side?

20) Name the two players who bowled in the series, but failed to take a wicket

21) Other than wicketkeepers, who took the most catches in the series?

22) Which four players were run-out in the series?

23) How many players were out stumped during the series?

24) How many wickets did Australia lose in the series?

25) How many wickets did England lose in the series?

26) Which six batsmen were dismissed for golden ducks during the series?

27) Which player was dismissed for a pair during the series?

28) Which England player made his 100th test match appearance in the first test?

29) What happened to the first ball Warner faced in the series?

30) Ben Stokes was denied a first test wicket, having forced which batsman to edge behind off a no-ball?

31) Who did Ben Stokes then dismiss in the 1st innings of the second test to claim his first test match wicket?

32) Which two players made their 100th test match appearances in the third test?

33) George Bailey ended Australia's 2nd innings of the third test by hitting 28 runs off an over bowled by who?

34) Which England player hit his first test match hundred as his side slipped towards defeat in the third test?

35) Which England bowler retired after the third test?

36) Who ran out Joe Root in the 2nd innings of the fourth test?

37) Who did Nathan Lyon dismiss in the fourth test to bring up 100 test match wickets?

38) Which Australian batsman brought up his 8000th test match run during the fourth test?

39) Which future England captain was dropped for the last test in the series?

40) Which English bowler made his test match debut in the fifth test, but could only complete 8.2 in the first innings after suffering an injury?

41) On the final day of the 5th test, which England batsman had his bat broken in half by a delivery from Ryan Harris?

42) Which Australian made his debut in the series, played every match, but was never picked for another test match?

2015

1) What was the result of the series?

2) Name the venue for each of the five tests

3) What was the result of each test?

4) From their initials, name every player who made an appearance for Australia during the series
M.C
B.H
J.H
M.J
N.L
M.M
S.M
P.N
C.R
P.S
S.S
M.S
A.V
D.W
S.W

5) From their initials, name every player who made an appearance for England during the series

M.A

J.A

J.B

G.B

I.B

S.B

J.B

A.C

S.F

A.L

J.R

B.S

M.W

6) Who were the head coaches of each side?

7) Who were the captains of each side?

8) Name the top 3 run scorers for Australia in the series

9) Name the top 3 run scorers for England in the series

10) Name the top 3 wicket-takers for Australia in the series

11) Name the top 3 wicket-takers for England in the series

12) Who won the man of the series award?

13) Which two Australians scored centuries in the series?

14) Which Englishman scored centuries in the series?

15) What was the highest partnership for each side in the series?

16) What was the highest total for each team in the series?

17) What was the lowest score each team was bowled out for in the series?

18) Who recorded the best match bowling figures for each side?

19) Who scored the highest individual score for each side?

20) Name the three players who bowled in the series, but failed to take a wicket

21) Other than wicketkeepers, who took the most catches in the series?

22) Who was the only player to be run-out in the series?

23) How many players were out stumped during the series?

24) How many wickets did Australia lose in the series?

25) How many wickets did England lose in the series?

26) Who was the only batsman to be dismissed for a golden duck during the series?

27) How many players were dismissed for pairs during the series?

28) Which two batsmen pulled England out of trouble with a 153 run partnership in the 1st innings of the first test?

29) Who took the final catch of the first match as England went 1-0 in the series?

30) Which Australian batsman retired hurt during the 2nd innings of the second test after suffering from dizziness?

31) Which England bowler returned to the side after a two year test absence to claim eight wickets in the third test?

32) Alastair Cook was caught after smashing the ball into the fielder at short leg who somehow clung onto the ball in the 1st innings of the third test, who was the fielder?

33) Which substitute fielder took the catch to dismiss Mitchell Starc as Australia built their lead in the 2nd innings at Edgbaston?

34) Who did Stuart Broad dismiss to claim his 300th test wicket during the fourth test?

35) Which Australian made his first ever test match duck in his 45th innings during the Trent Bridge test?

36) Ben Stokes took a spectacular one-handed catch to dismiss which batsman in the 1st innings of the fourth test?

37) How many Australian batsman made double figure scores as they were bowled out for 60 at Trent Bridge?

38) How many overs did Australia bat for in their 1st innings at Trent Bridge?

39) Who bowled Nathan Lyon in the 2nd innings at Trent Bridge to secure the Ashes for England?

40) Who was the last batman dismissed in the series?

41) Which two Australian batsman retired from test cricket after the series?

2017/18

1) What was the result of the series?

2) Name the venue for each of the five tests

3) What was the result of each test?

4) From their initials, name every player who made
   an appearance for Australia during the series
   C.B
   J.B
   P.C
   P.H
   J.H
   U.K
   N.L
   M.M
   S.M
   T.P
   S.S
   M.S
   D.W

5) From their initials, name every player who made an appearance for England during the series

M.A

J.A

J.B

J.B

S.B

A.C

M.C

T.C

D.M

C.O

J.R

M.S

C.W

J.V

6) Who were the head coaches of each side?

7) Who were the captains of each side?

8) Name the top 3 run scorers for Australia in the series

9) Name the top 3 run scorers for England in the series

10) Name the top 3 wicket-takers for Australia in the series

11) Name the top 3 wicket-takers for England in the series

12) Who won the man of the series award?

13) Which five Australians scored centuries in the series?

14) Which three Englishmen scored centuries in the series?

15) What was the highest partnership for each side in the series?

16) What was the highest total for each team in the series?

17) What was the lowest score each team was bowled out for in the series?

18) Who recorded the best match bowling figures for each side?

19) Who scored the highest individual score for each side?

20) Name the four players who bowled in the series, but failed to take a wicket

21) Other than wicketkeepers, who took the most catches in the series?

22) Which players were run-out in the series?

23) Which two players were out stumped during the series?

24) How many wickets did Australia lose in the series?

25) How many wickets did England lose in the series?

26) How many batsmen were dismissed for golden ducks during the series?

27) How many players were dismissed for pairs during the series?

28) The 2017/18 series featured the first ever day/night match in Ashes history, at which ground?

29) Which England player missed the series because he was serving a suspension after being recorded fighting outside a bar?

30) Mitchell Starc bowled which England batsman in the 2nd innings of the third test with a ball which deviated wickedly off a crack in the pitch?

31) Which England batsman was stumped by millimetres in their 2nd innings of the first test?

32) Craig Overton took the wicket of who to claim his first test scalp?

33) Who took his first ever 5 wicket haul in Australia in the second test?

34) In their 1st innings of the second test, England lost three consecutive wickets by being caught and bowled, which three batsmen were dismissed and by who?

35) Who was the last man out as Australia bowled out England to regain the Ashes in the third test?

36) Tom Curran thought he had his first test wicket, but which batsman was reprieved when it was shown to be a no-ball?

37) Who did Tom Curran then dismiss to claim his maiden test match victim?

38) Steve Smith took a stunning one-handed slip catch to dismiss who in the 1st innings of the fifth test?

39) Moeen Ali was given a life after which Australian dropped an easy chance as the ball lobbed to him at midwicket in the 1st innings of the fifth test?

40) Mason Crane was denied his first test wicket having bowled a no-ball in trapping which batsman LBW?

41) Who did later become Mason Crane's first test match wicket?

42) Who was the last man to be dismissed in the series?

2019

1) What was the result of the series?

2) Name the venue for each of the five tests

3) What was the result of each test?

4) From their initials, name every player who made
   an appearance for Australia during the series
   C.B
   P.C
   M.H
   J.H
   T.H
   U.K
   M.L
   N.L
   M.M
   T.P
   J.P
   P.S
   S.S
   M.S
   M.W
   D.W

5) From their initials, name every player who made an appearance for England during the series

M.A

J.A

J.A

J.B

S.B

R.B

J.B

S.C

J.D

J.L

C.O

J.R

J.R

B.S

C.W

6) Who were the head coaches of each side?

7) Who were the captains of each side?

8) Name the top 3 run scorers for Australia in the series

9) Name the top 3 run scorers for England in the series

10) Name the top 3 wicket-takers for Australia in the series

11) Name the top 3 wicket-takers for England in the series

12) Who won the man of the series award?

13) Which two Australians scored centuries in the series?

14) Which two Englishmen scored centuries in the series?

15) What was the highest partnership for each side in the series?

16) What was the highest total for each team in the series?

17) What was the lowest score each team was bowled out for in the series?

18) Who recorded the best match bowling figures for each side?

19) Who scored the highest individual score for each side?

20) Name the five players who bowled in the series, but failed to take a wicket

21) Other than wicketkeepers, who took the most catches in the series?

22) Which two players were run-out in the series?

23) Which two players were out stumped during the series?

24) How many wickets did Australia lose in the series?

25) How many wickets did England lose in the series?

26) Which four batsmen were dismissed for golden ducks during the series?

27) Which player registered the only pair of the series?

28) Who did England face in a test match one week before the start of the Ashes?

29) Steve Smith, David Warner and Cameron Bancroft returned to the Australian test squad for the first time since serving bans for the ball tampering incident against which team?

30) The previous meeting between England and Australia was in the semi-final of the world cup, what was the result?

31) Who did Stuart Broad dismiss to claim his 450th test match wicket during the series?

32) Who did Pat Cummins claim as his 100th test match wicket during the series?

33) Nathan Lyon reached 350 test match wickets by dismissing who?

34) Nathan Lyon moved above Dennis Lillee into 3rd place on the all-time list of Australian wicket-takers by dismissing who?

35) The 2019 series was the first Ashes series in which players had their names and squad numbers on the back of their shirts – can you name the following players from their squad number?
England:
66
22
9

Australia:
1
31
49

36) Which two Sky Sports commentators, both former England captains, made their final appearances for the broadcaster in the series?

37) How many hundreds did Steve Smith Score in the series?

38) How many times did Stuart Broad dismiss David Warner?

39) Who bowled the first ball of the series?

40) Who took the first wicket in the series?

41) How many overs did Jimmy Anderson bowl in the series?

42) Jofra Archer made his test match debut at Lord's, who did he dismiss for his first test match wicket?

43) Who became the first ever concussion substitute in a test match during the second test?

44) Nathan Lyon missed a clear chance to win the third test with a run out, but which batsman was he attempting to dismiss?

45) Which umpire incorrectly gave Ben Stokes not out when England required just 2 runs for victory at Headingley?

46) Who claimed their only wicket of the series to dismiss Jack Leach in the closing stages of the fourth test as Australia neared victory?

47) Who was England's last man out as Australia retained the Ashes?

48) Who bowled the last ball of the series?

Decade Records

1) Who made the most appearances for Australia across the decade?

2) Who made the most appearances for England across the decade?

3) Who made the most appearances for either side as captain across the decade?

4) Who scored the most runs for Australia across the decade?

5) Who scored the most runs for England across the decade?

6) Who took the most wickets for Australia across the decade?

7) Who took the most wickets for England across the decade?

8) How many Ashes hundreds did Alastair Cook score in England?

9) At the end of the 2015 series, how many Ashes series had Ian Bell won with England in his career?

10) What was total score in matches between the sides across the decade?

Answers – 2010/11

1) What was the result of the series?
   England won 3-1

2) Name the venue for each of the five tests
   1st Wooloongabba Cricket Ground, Brisbane
   2nd Adelaide Oval
   3rd Western Australia Cricket Association Ground, Perth
   4th Melbourne Cricket Ground
   5th Sydney Cricket Ground

3) What was the result of each test?
   1st Test – Draw
   2nd Test – England win
   3rd Test – Australia win
   4th Test – England win
   5th Test – England win

4) From their initials, name every player who made an appearance for Australia during the series

Michael Beer
Doug Bollinger
Michael Clarke
Xavier Doherty
Brad Haddin
Ryan Harris
Ben Hilfenhaus
Phillip Hughes
Michael Hussey
Mitchell Johnson
Simon Katich
Usman Khawaja
Marcus North
Ricky Ponting
Peter Siddle
Steve Smith
Shane Watson

5) From their initials, name every player who made an appearance for England during the series
James Anderson
Ian Bell
Tim Bresnan
Stuart Broad
Paul Collingwood
Alastair Cook
Steven Finn
Kevin Pietersen
Matt Prior
Andrew Strauss
Graeme Swann
Chris Tremlett
Jonathan Trott

6) Who were the head coaches of each side?
Australia – Tim Neilsen
England – Andy Flower

7) Who were the captains of each side?
Australia – Ricky Ponting and Michael Clarke (5th Test only)
England – Andrew Strauss

8) Name the top 3 run scorers for Australia in the series
   Michael Hussey – 570
   Shane Watson – 435
   Brad Haddin – 360

9) Name the top 3 run scorers for England in the series
   Alastair Cook – 766
   Jonathan Trott – 445
   Kevin Pietersen – 360

10) Name the top 3 wicket-takers for Australia in the series
   Mitchell Johnson – 15
   Peter Siddle – 14
   Ryan Harris – 11

11) Name the top 3 wicket-takers for England in the series
   James Anderson – 24
   Chris Tremlett – 17
   Graeme Swann – 15

12) Who won the man of the series award?
   Alastair Cook

13) Which two Australians scored centuries in the series?
   Michael Hussey (2)
   Brad Haddin

14) Which six Englishmen scored centuries in the series?
   Alastair Cook (3)
   Kevin Pietersen (1)
   Jonathan Trott (2)
   Matt Prior
   Ian Bell
   Andrew Strauss

15) What was the highest partnership for each side in the series?
   Australia – Michael Hussey and Brad Haddin – 307 for the 6th wicket at Brisbane 1st innings
   England – Cook and Trott – 329* for the 2nd wicket at Brisbane 2nd innings

16) What was the highest total for each team in the series?
   Australia – 481 1st innings at Brisbane
   England – 644 1st innings at Sydney

17) What was the lowest score each team was bowled out for in the series?
Australia – 98 1st innings at Melbourne
England – 123 2nd innings at Perth

18) Who recorded the best match bowling figures for each sides?
Mitchell Johnson – 29.3-8-82-9 at Perth
Chris Tremlett – 47.0-7-150-8 at Perth

19) Who scored the highest individual score for each side?
Australia – Michael Hussey 195 1st innings at Brisbane
England – Alastair Cook 235* 2nd innings at Brisbane

20) Name the three players who bowled in the series, but failed to take a wicket
Michael Hussey
Michael Clarke
Steve Smith

21) Other than wicketkeepers, who took the most catches in the series?
Paul Collingwood - 9

22) Which four players were run-out in the series?
Simon Katich – 1st innings at Adelaide
Xavier Doherty – 1st innings at Adelaide
Phillip Hughes – 2nd innings at Melbourne
Shane Watson – 2nd innings at Sydney

23) Which players were out stumped during the series?
Andrew Strauss – 2nd innings at Brisbane

24) How many wickets did Australia lose in the series?
91

25) How many wickets did England lose in the series?
56

26) Which five batsmen were dismissed for golden ducks during the series?
Matt Prior – 1st innings at Brisbane
Stuart Broad – 1st innings at Brisbane
Ricky Ponting – 1st innings at Adelaide
Ryan Harris – 1st and 2nd innings at Adelaide
Mitchell Johnson – 2nd innings at Sydney

27) Which two players were dismissed for pairs during the series?

Ryan Harris – at Adelaide
Ben Hilfenhaus – at Melbourne

28) Which now common-place system was used in the Ashes for the first time in this series?

The Review System

29) Who took a hat-trick on his birthday, during the first test?

Peter Siddle

30) Xaiver Doherty dismissed who to claim his first test wicket during the first test?

Ian Bell

31) Andrew Strauss narrowly avoided a pair when he was struck on the pads leaving the first ball of the second innings. Who was the bowler?

Ben Hilfenhaus

32) What did England declare on in the 2nd innings of the first test?

517/1

33) Who dismissed Michael Clarke with the last ball of the fourth day of the second test to help push England towards victory?
Kevin Pietersen

34) Simon Katich was run-out in the 1st over of the second test without facing a ball, which England fielder threw down the stumps?
Jonathan Trott

35) Who did James Anderson dismiss in the 2nd innings of the third test for his 200th test wicket?
Peter Siddle

36) Which future England one-day captain appeared as a substitute fielder during the series?
Eoin Morgan

37) Who did England drop for the fourth test, despite him being the leading wicket-taker in the series at that point?
Steven Finn

38) Who was the last man out for Australia when England retained the Ashes during the fourth test?

Ben Hilfenhaus

39) Who did Paul Collingwood's dismiss for his final ever test wicket in the 1st innings of the fifth test?

Michael Hussey

40) During the fifth test Alastair Cook became the second youngest player to reach 5000 runs, who was the only player younger than him to achieve this landmark?

Sachin Tendulkar

41) Michael Beer was denied his first test match wicket for what reason when Alastair Cook was caught on 47 during the fifth test?

It was a no ball

42) Michael Beer was again denied his first test match wicket when the Australians appealed for a catch when Cook was on 99, for what reason was the wicket not given?
The ball bounced before the catch was taken by short leg

43) Michael Beer finally claimed his first test wicket, and in doing so dismissed which England player who was playing his final ever test match?
Paul Collingwood

44) Who was the not out batsman in the fifth test as England bowled Australia out to clinch the series?
Steve Smith

Answers – 2013

1) What was the result of the series?
   England won 3-0

2) Name the venue for each of the five tests
   1st Trent Bridge, Nottingham
   2nd Lord's, London
   3rd Old Trafford, Manchester
   4th Riverside Ground, Chester-le-Street
   5th The Oval, London

3) What was the result of each test?
   1st Test – England win
   2nd Test – England win
   3rd Test – Draw
   4th Test – England win
   5th Test – Draw

4) From their initials, name every player who made an appearance for Australia during the series

Ashton Agar
Jackson Bird
Michael Clarke
Ed Cowan
James Faulkner
Brad Haddin
Ryan Harris
Phillip Hughes
Usman Khawaja
Nathan Lyon
James Pattinson
Chris Rogers
Peter Siddle
Steve Smith
Mitchell Starc
David Warner
Shane Watson

5) From their initials, name every player who made an appearance for England during the series

James Anderson
Jonny Bairstow
Ian Bell
Tim Bresnan
Stuart Broad
Alastair Cook
Steven Finn
Simon Kerrigan
Kevin Pietersen
Matt Prior
Joe Root
Graeme Swann
Jonathan Trott
Chris Woakes

6) Who were the head coaches of each side?
Australia – Darren Lehmann
England – Andy Flower

7) Who were the captains of each side?
Australia – Michael Clarke
England – Alastair Cook

8) Name the top 3 run scorers for Australia in the series
Shane Watson 418
Michael Clarke 381
Chris Rogers 367

9) Name the top 3 run scorers for England in the series
Ian Bell – 562
Kevin Pietersen – 388
Joe Root – 339

10) Name the top 3 wicket-takers for Australia in the series

Ryan Harris – 24
Peter Siddle – 17
Mitchell Starc – 11

11) Name the top 3 wicket-takers for England in the series
Graeme Swann – 26
Stuart Broad – 22
James Anderson – 22

12) Who won the man of the series award?
Ian Bell

13) Which four Australians scored centuries in the series?
Michael Clarke
Shane Watson
Chris Rogers
Steve Smith

14) Which three Englishmen scored centuries in the series?
Joe Root
Kevin Pietersen
Ian Bell (3)

15) What was the highest partnership for each side in the series?
Australia – Michael Clarke and Steve Smith – 214 for the 4th wicket at Old Trafford 1st innings
England – Joe Root and Ian Bell – 153 for the 5th wicket at Lord's 2nd innings

16) What was the highest total for each team in the series?
Australia – 527/7 1st innings at Old Trafford
England – 377 1st innings at The Oval

17) What was the lowest score each team was bowled out for in the series?
Australia – 128 1st innings at Lord's
England – 215 1st innings at Trent Bridge

18) Who recorded the best match bowling figures for each side?
Australia – Ryan Harris – 47.0-5-187-9 at Chester-le-Street
England – Stuart Broad – 43.0-10-121-11 at Chester-le-Street

19) Who scored the highest individual score for each side?
Australia – Michael Clarke 187 1st innings at Old Trafford
England – Joe Root 180 2nd innings at Lord's

20) Name the two players who bowled in the series, but failed to take a wicket
Michael Clarke
Simon Kerrigan

21) Other than wicketkeepers, who took the most catches in the series?
Alastair Cook – 7

22) Which players were run-out in the series?
Ashton Agar – 1st innings at Lord's
Steve Smith – 2nd innings at Old Trafford
Ian Bell – 2nd innings at The Oval

23) How many players were out stumped during the series?
0

24) How many wickets did Australia lose in the series?
89

25) How many wickets did England lose in the series?
85

26) Which five batsmen were dismissed for golden ducks during the series?
Steven Finn – 1st innings at Trent Bridge
Ed Cowan – 1st innings at Trent Bridge
Jonathan Trott – 2nd innings at Trent Bridge
Matt Prior – 2nd innings at Chester-le-Street
Brad Haddin – 2nd innings at The Oval

27) How many players were dismissed for pairs during the series?

0

28) Who was sacked as Australia's coach just before the start of the series?

Mickey Arthur

29) David Warner was serving a ban up until the first test after punching who in bar earlier in the summer?

Joe Root

30) James Pattinson bowled the first ball of the series, what happened?

It was a wide

31) How many runs did Philip Hughes and Ashton Agar add for the 10th wicket in the 1st innings of the first test?

163

32) Ashton Agar made what score batting at number 11 in his first ever test innings?

98

33) Stuart Broad infamously refused to walk and was given not-out after edging to first slip off the bowling of which Australian in the 2nd innings of the first test?
Ashton Agar

34) Which Australian hit his maiden test match hundred during the 4th test?
Chris Rogers

35) Steve Smith secured his first test match century by hitting which bowler for 6 during the fifth test?
Jonathan Trott

36) Which two English bowlers made their test match debuts in the fifth test?
Chris Woakes and Simon Kerrigan

37) What happened to the first ball Chris Woakes faced in test cricket?
He hit it for four

38) Chris Woakes had his first test wicket taken off him after which Australian successfully reviewed an LBW decision?
Shane Watson

39) Which Australian all-rounder made his test match debut in the fifth test?
James Faulkner

40) Brad Haddin claimed a world record by taking how many catches in the series?
29

Answers – 2013/14

1) What was the result of the series?
   Australia won 5-0

2) Name the venue for each of the five tests
   1st Wooloongabba Cricket Ground, Brisbane
   2nd Adelaide Oval
   3rd Western Australia Cricket Association
   Ground, Perth
   4th Melbourne Cricket Ground
   5th Sydney Cricket Ground

3) What was the result of each test?
   1st Test – Australia win
   2nd Test – Australia win
   3rd Test – Australia win
   4th Test – Australia win
   5th Test – Australia win

4) From their initials, name every player who made an appearance for Australia during the series

George Bailey
Michael Clarke
Brad Haddin
Ryan Harris
Mitchell Johnson
Nathan Lyon
Chris Rogers
Peter Siddle
Steve Smith
David Warner
Shane Watson

5) From their initials, name every player who made an appearance for England during the series
James Anderson
Jonny Bairstow
Gary Ballance
Ian Bell
Scott Borthwick
Tim Bresnan
Stuart Broad
Michael Carberry
Alastair Cook
Steven Finn
Monty Panesar
Kevin Pietersen
Matt Prior
Boyd Rankin
Joe Root
Ben Stokes
Graeme Swann
Chris Tremlett
Jonathan Trott

6) Who were the head coaches of each side?
Australia – Darren Lehmann
England – Andy Flower

7) Who were the captains of each side?
   Australia – Michael Clarke
   England – Alastair Cook

8) Name the top 3 run scorers for Australia in the series
   David Warner – 523
   Brad Haddin – 493
   Chris Rogers – 463

9) Name the top 3 run scorers for England in the series
   Kevin Pietersen – 294
   Michael Carberry – 281
   Ben Stokes – 279

10) Name the top 3 wicket-takers for Australia in the series

    Mitchell Johnson – 37
    Ryan Harris – 22
    Nathan Lyon – 19

11) Name the top 3 wicket-takers for England in the series
    Stuart Broad – 21
    Ben Stokes – 15
    James Anderson – 14

12) Who won the man of the series award?
Mitchell Johnson

13) Which six Australians scored centuries in the series?
Michael Clarke (2)
David Warner (2)
Chris Rogers (2)
Brad Haddin
Steve Smith (2)
Shane Watson

14) Which Englishman scored a century in the series?
Ben Stokes

15) What was the highest partnership for each side in the series?
Australia – Michael Clarke and Brad Haddin – 200 for the 6th wicket at Adelaide 1st innings
England – Joe Root and Kevin Pietersen – 111 for the 3rd wicket at Adelaide 2nd innings

16) What was the highest total for each team in the series?
Australia – 570/9 1st innings at Adelaide
England – 353 4th innings at Perth

17) What was the lowest score each team was bowled out for in the series?
Australia – 204 1st innings at Melbourne
England – 136 1st innings at Brisbane

18) Who recorded the best match bowling figures for each side?
Australia – Mitchell Johnson – 38.1-9-103-9 at Brisbane
England – Stuart Broad – 40.0-7-136-8 at Brisbane

19) Who scored the highest individual score for each side?
Australia – Michael Clarke – 148 1st innings at Adelaide
England – Ben Stokes – 120 2nd innings at Perth

20) Name the two players who bowled in the series, but failed to take a wicket
Kevin Pietersen
Joe Root

21) Other than wicketkeepers, who took the most catches in the series?
George Bailey – 10

22) Which four players were run-out in the series?
   Brad Haddin – 1st innings at Brisbane
   Chris Rogers – 1st innings at Perth
   Shane Watson – 2nd innings at Perth
   Joe Root – 2nd innings at Melbourne

23) How many players were out stumped during the series?
   0

24) How many wickets did Australia lose in the series?
   77

25) How many wickets did England lose in the series?
   100

26) Which six batsmen were dismissed for golden ducks during the series?
   Matt Prior – 1st innings at Brisbane
   Stuart Broad – 1st innings at Adelaide
   James Anderson – 1st innings at Adelaide
   Alastair Cook – 2nd innings at Perth
   Ian Bell – 2nd innings at Melbourne
   Peter Siddle – 1st innings at Sydney

27) Which player was dismissed for a pair during the series?
Graeme Swann – at Brisbane

28) Which England player made his 100th test match appearance in the first test?
Kevin Pietersen

29) What happened to the first ball Warner faced in the series?
He hooked it for four off Stuart Broad

30) Ben Stokes was denied a first test wicket, having forced which batsman to edge behind off a no-ball?
Brad Haddin

31) Who did Ben Stokes then dismiss in the 1st innings of the second test to claim his first test match wicket?
Michael Clarke

32) Which two players made their 100th test match appearances in the third test?
Michael Clarke and Alastair Cook

33) George Bailey ended Australia's 2nd innings of the third test by hitting 28 runs off an over bowled by who?
James Anderson

34) Which England player hit his first test match hundred as his side slipped towards defeat in the third test?
Ben Stokes

35) Which England bowler retired after the third test?
Graeme Swann

36) Who ran out Joe Root in the 2nd innings of the fourth test?
Mitchell Johnson

37) Who did Nathan Lyon dismiss in the fourth test to bring up 100 test match wickets?
Stuart Broad

38) Which Australian batsman brought up his 8000th test match run during the fourth test?
Michael Clarke

39) Which future England captain was dropped for the last test in the series?
Joe Root

40) Which English bowler made his test match debut in the fifth test, but could only complete 8.2 in the first innings after suffering an injury?
Boyd Rankin

41) On the final day of the 5th test, which England batsman had his bat broken in half by a delivery from Ryan Harris?
Michael Carberry

42) Which Australian made his debut in the series, played every match, but was never picked for another test match?
George Bailey

Answers – 2015

1) What was the result of the series?
   England won 3-2

2) Name the venue for each of the five tests
   1st Sophia Gardens, Cardiff
   2nd Lord's, London
   3rd Edgbaston, Birmingham
   4th Trent Bridge, Nottingham
   5th The Oval, London

3) What was the result of each test?
   1st Test – England win
   2nd Test – Australia win
   3rd Test – England win
   4th Test – England win
   5th Test – Australia win

4) From their initials, name every player who made an appearance for Australia during the series

Michael Clarke
Brad Haddin
Josh Hazlewood
Mitchell Johnson
Nathan Lyon
Mitchell Marsh
Shaun Marsh
Peter Nevill
Chris Rogers
Peter Siddle
Steve Smith
Mitchell Starc
Adam Voges
David Warner
Shane Watson

5) From their initials, name every player who made an appearance for England during the series

Moeen Ali

James Anderson

Jonny Bairstow

Gary Ballance

Ian Bell

Stuart Broad

Jos Buttler

Alastair Cook

Steven Finn

Adam Lyth

Joe Root

Ben Stokes

Mark Wood

6) Who were the head coaches of each side?

Australia – Darren Lehmann

England – Trevor Bayliss

7) Who were the captains of each side?

Australia – Michael Clarke

England – Alastair Cook

8) Name the top 3 run scorers for Australia in the series
Steve Smith – 508
Chris Rogers – 480
David Warner – 418

9) Name the top 3 run scorers for England in the series
Joe Root – 460
Alastair Cook – 330
Moeen Ali – 293

10) Name the top 3 wicket-takers for Australia in the series
Mitchell Starc – 18
Josh Hazlewood – 16
Nathan Lyon – 16

11) Name the top 3 wicket-takers for England in the series
Stuart Broad – 21
Steven Finn – 12
Moeen Ali – 12

12) Who won the man of the series award?
Joe Root

13) Which two Australians scored centuries in the series?
Steve Smith (2)
Chris Rogers

14) Which Englishman scored centuries in the series?
Joe Root (2)

15) What was the highest partnership for each side in the series?
Australia – Chris Rogers and Steve Smith – 284 for the 2nd wicket at Lord's 1st innings
England – Joe Root and Jonny Bairstow – 173 for the 4th wicket at Trent Bridge 1st innings

16) What was the highest total for each team in the series?
Australia – 566/8 1st innings at Lord's
England – 430 1st innings at Cardiff

17) What was the lowest score each team was bowled out for in the series?
Australia – 60 1st innings at Trent Bridge
England – 103 2nd innings at Lord's

18) Who recorded the best match bowling figures for each side?

Australia – Mitchell Starc – 40.1-8-174-7 at Cardiff

England – Stuart Broad – 25.3-10-51-9 at Trent Bridge

19) Who scored the highest individual score for each side?

Australia – Steve Smith 215 – 1st innings at Lord's

England – Joe Root – 134 1st innings at Cardiff

20) Name the three players who bowled in the series, but failed to take a wicket

Adam Lyth

David Warner

Shane Watson

21) Other than wicketkeepers, who took the most catches in the series?

Alastair Cook - 9

22) Who was the only player to be run-out in the series?

Ben Stokes – 2nd innings at Lord's

23) How many players were out stumped during the series?

0

24) How many wickets did Australia lose in the series?

80

25) How many wickets did England lose in the series?

81

26) Who was the only batsman to be dismissed for a golden duck during the series?

Adam Voges – 2ⁿᵈ innings at Edgbaston

27) How many players were dismissed for pairs during the series?

0

28) Which two batsmen pulled England out of trouble with a 153 run partnership in the 1ˢᵗ innings of the first test?

Gary Ballance and Joe Root

29) Who took the final catch of the first match as England went 1-0 in the series?

Joe Root

30) Which Australian batsman retired hurt during the 2nd innings of the second test after suffering from dizziness?

Chris Rogers

31) Which England bowler returned to the side after a two year test absence to claim eight wickets in the third test?

Steven Finn

32) Alastair Cook was caught after smashing the ball into the fielder at short leg who somehow clung onto the ball in the 1st innings of the third test, who was the fielder?

Adam Voges

33) Which substitute fielder took the catch to dismiss Mitchell Starc as Australia built their lead in the 2nd innings at Edgbaston?

Josh Poysden

34) Who did Stuart Broad dismiss to claim his 300th test wicket during the fourth test?

Chris Rogers

35) Which Australian made his first ever test match duck in his 45th innings during the Trent Bridge test?

Chris Rogers

36) Ben Stokes took a spectacular one-handed catch to dismiss which batsman in the 1st innings of the fourth test?

Adam Voges

37) How many Australian batsman made double figure scores as they were bowled out for 60 at Trent Bridge?

2 – Michael Clarke (10) and Mitchell Johnson (13)

38) How many overs did Australia bat for in their 1st innings at Trent Bridge?

18.3

39) Who bowled Nathan Lyon in the 2nd innings at Trent Bridge to secure the Ashes for England?

Mark Wood

40) Who was the last batman dismissed in the series?

Moeen Ali – caught behind off Peter Siddle

41) Which two Australian batsman retired from test cricket after the series?

Chris Rogers and Michael Clarke

Answers – 2017/18

1) What was the result of the series?
Australia won 4-0

2) Name the venue for each of the five tests
1st Wooloongabba Cricket Ground, Brisbane
2nd Adelaide Oval
3rd Western Australia Cricket Association Ground, Perth
4th Melbourne Cricket Ground
5th Sydney Cricket Ground

3) What was the result of each test?
1st Test – Australia win
2nd Test – Australia win
3rd Test – Australia win
4th Test – draw
5th Test – Australia win

4) From their initials, name every player who made an appearance for Australia during the series

Cameron Bancroft

Jackson Bird

Pat Cummins

Peter Handscomb

Josh Hazlewood

Usman Khawaja

Nathan Lyon

Mitchell Marsh

Shaun Marsh

Tim Paine

Steve Smith

Mitchell Starc

David Warner

5) From their initials, name every player who made an appearance for England during the series
   Moeen Ali
   James Anderson
   Jonny Bairstow
   Jake Ball
   Stuart Broad
   Alastair Cook
   Mason Crane
   Tom Curran
   Dawid Malan
   Craig Overton
   Joe Root
   Mark Stoneman
   Chris Woakes
   James Vince

6) Who were the head coaches of each side?
   Australia – Darren Lehmann
   England – Trevor Bayliss

7) Who were the captains of each side?
   Australia – Steve Smith
   England – Joe Root

8) Name the top 3 run scorers for Australia in the series
Steve Smith – 687
Shaun Marsh – 445
David Warner – 441

9) Name the top 3 run scorers for England in the series
Dawid Malan – 383
Joe Root – 378
Alastair Cook – 376

10) Name the top 3 wicket-takers for Australia in the series
Pat Cummins – 23
Mitchell Starc – 22
Josh Hazlewood and Nathan Lyon – 21

11) Name the top 3 wicket-takers for England in the series
James Anderson – 17
Stuart Broad – 11
Chris Woakes – 10

12) Who won the man of the series award?
Steve Smith

13) Which five Australians scored centuries in the series?
Steve Smith (3)
Shaun Marsh (2)
Mitchell Marsh (2)
David Warner
Usman Khawaja

14) Which three Englishmen scored centuries in the series?
Dawid Malan
Alastair Cook
Jonny Bairstow

15) What was the highest partnership for each side in the series?
Australia – Steve Smith and Mitchell Marsh – 301 for the 5th wicket at Perth 1st innings
England – Dawid Malan and Jonny Bairstow – 237 for the 5th wicket at Perth 1st innings

16) What was the highest total for each team in the series?
Australia – 662/9 1st innings at Perth
England – 491 1st innings at Melbourne

17) What was the lowest score each team was bowled out for in the series?
Australia – 138 2nd innings at Adelaide
England – 180 2nd innings at Sydney

18) Who recorded the best match bowling figures for each side?
Australia – Pat Cummins – 41.3-9-119-8 at Sydney
England – James Anderson – 53.0-12-117-6 at Adelaide

19) Who scored the highest individual score for each side?
Australia – Steve Smith – 239 1st innings at Perth
England – Alastair Cook – 244* 1st innings at Melbourne

20) Name the four players who bowled in the series, but failed to take a wicket
Steve Smith
Jackson Bird
Mitchell Marsh
Dawid Malan

21) Other than wicketkeepers, who took the most catches in the series?
Steve Smith – 10

22) Which players were run-out in the series?
James Vince – 1st innings at Brisbane
Cameron Bancroft – 1st innings at Adelaide
Mitchell Starc – 1st innings at Perth
Mason Crane – 1st innings at Sydney
Shaun Marsh – 1st innings at Sydney

23) Which two players were out stumped during the series?
Moeen Ali – 2nd innings at Brisbane
Usman Khawaja – 1st innings at Sydney

24) How many wickets did Australia lose in the series?
58

25) How many wickets did England lose in the series?
90

26) How many batsmen were dismissed for golden ducks during the series?
0

27) How many players were dismissed for pairs during the series?

0

28) The 2017/18 series featured the first ever day/night match in Ashes history, at which ground?

Adelaide

29) Which England player missed the series because he was serving a suspension after being recorded fighting outside a bar?

Ben Stokes

30) Mitchell Starc bowled which England batsman in the 2nd innings of the third test with a ball which deviated wickedly off a crack in the pitch?

James Vince

31) Which England batsman was stumped by millimetres in their 2nd innings of the first test?

Moeen Ali

32) Craig Overton took the wicket of who to claim his first test scalp?

Steve Smith

33) Who took his first ever 5 wicket haul in Australia in the second test?
James Anderson

34) In their 1st innings of the second test, England lost three consecutive wickets by being caught and bowled, which three batsmen were dismissed and by who?
Moeen Ali – c&b Lyon
Jonny Bairstow – c&b Starc
Chris Woakes – c&b Starc

35) Who was the last man out as Australia bowled out England to regain the Ashes in the third test?
Chris Woakes

36) Tom Curran thought he had his first test wicket, but which batsman was reprieved when it was shown to be a no-ball?
David Warner

37) Who did Tom Curran then dismiss to claim his maiden test match victim?
Steve Smith

38) Steve Smith took a stunning one-handed slip catch to dismiss who in the 1st innings of the fifth test?

Dawid Malan

39) Moeen Ali was given a life after which Australian dropped an easy chance as the ball lobbed to him at midwicket in the 1st innings of the fifth test?

Josh Hazlewood

40) Mason Crane was denied his first test wicket having bowled a no-ball in trapping which batsman LBW?

Usman Khawaja

41) Who did later become Mason Crane's first test match wicket?

Usman Khawaja

42) Who was the last man to be dismissed in the series?

James Anderson – caught behind off Josh Hazlewood

Answers – 2019

1) What was the result of the series?
   2-2

2) Name the venue for each of the five tests
   1st Edgbaston, Birmingham
   2nd Lord's, London
   3rd Headingley, Leeds
   4th Old Trafford, Manchester
   5th The Oval, London

3) What was the result of each test?
   1st Test – Australia win
   2nd Test – draw
   3rd Test – England win
   4th Test – Australia win
   5th Test – England win

4) From their initials, name every player who made an appearance for Australia during the series

Cameron Bancroft
Pat Cummins
Marcus Harris
Josh Hazlewood
Travis Head
Usman Khawaja
Marnus Labuschagne
Nathan Lyon
Mitchell Marsh
Tim Paine
James Pattinson
Peter Siddle
Steve Smith
Mitchell Starc
Matthew Wade
David Warner

5) From their initials, name every player who made an appearance for England during the series
Moeen Ali
James Anderson
Jofra Archer
Jonny Bairstow
Stuart Broad
Rory Burns
Jos Buttler
Sam Curran
Joe Denly
Jack Leach
Craig Overton
Joe Root
Jason Roy
Ben Stokes
Chris Woakes

6) Who were the head coaches of each side?
Australia – Justin Langer
England – Trevor Bayliss

7) Who were the captains of each side?
Australia – Tim Paine
England – Joe Root

8) Name the top 3 run scorers for Australia in the series
Steve Smith - 774
Marnus Labuschage - 353
Matthew Wade – 337

9) Name the top 3 run scorers for England in the series
Ben Stokes - 441
Rory Burns - 390
Joe Root - 325

10) Name the top 3 wicket-takers for Australia in the series
Pat Cummins - 29
Josh Hazlewood - 20
Nathan Lyon – 20

11) Name the top 3 wicket-takers for England in the series
Stuart Broad - 23
Jofra Archer - 22
Jack Leach - 12

12) Who won the man of the series award?
Steve Smith

13) Which two Australians scored centuries in the series?
Steve Smith (3)
Matthew Wade (2)

14) Which two Englishmen scored centuries in the series?
Ben Stokes (2)
Rory Burns

15) What was the highest partnership for each side in the series?
Australia - 145 for the 6th wicket between Steve Smith and Tim Paine 1st innings Old Trafford
England - 141 for the 3rd wicket between Joe Root and Rory Burns 1st innings Old Trafford

16) What was the highest total for each team in the series?
Australia - 497/8 1st innings Old Trafford
England – 374 2nd innings Edgbaston

17) What was the lowest score each team was bowled out for in the series?
Australia – 179 1st innings Headingley
England – 67 1st innings Headingley

18) Who recorded the best match bowling figures for each side?

Australia – Josh Hazlewood 43.5-13-115-9 Headingley

England – Jofra Archer 31.1-5-85-8 Headingley

19) Who scored the highest individual score for each side?

Australia – Steve Smith 211 1st innings Old Trafford

England – Ben Stokes 135no 2nd innings Headingley

20) Name the five players who bowled in the series, but failed to take a wicket

James Anderson
Joe Denly
Travis Head
Matthew Wade
Steve Smith

21) Other than wicketkeepers, who took the most catches in the series?

Steve Smith – 12

22) Which two players were run-out in the series?
Marnus Labuschagne – 2nd innings at Headingley
Jos Buttler – 2nd innings at Headingley

23) Which two players were out stumped during the series?
Marnus Labuschagne and Matthew Wade in the 2nd innings at The Oval

24) How many wickets did Australia lose in the series?
87

25) How many wickets did England lose in the series?
94

26) Which four batsmen were dismissed for golden ducks during the series?
Stuart Broad by Nathan Lyon – 2nd innings at Edgbaston
Joe Root – 2nd innings at Lord's and 2nd innings at Old Trafford
Pat Cummins – 1st innings at The Oval
Josh Hazlewood – 2nd innings at The Oval

27) Which player registered the only pair of the series?
David Warner at Old Trafford

28) Who did England face in a test match one week before the start of the Ashes?
Ireland

29) Steve Smith, David Warner and Cameron Bancroft returned to the Australian test squad for the first time since serving bans for the ball-tampering incident against which team?
South Africa

30) The previous meeting between England and Australia was in the semi-final of the world cup, what was the result?
England won by 8 wickets

31) Who did Stuart Broad dismiss to claim his 450th test match wicket during the series?
David Warner – 2nd innings at Edgbaston

32) Who did Pat Cummins claim as his 100th test match wicket during the series?
Jonny Bairstow – 2nd innings at Edgbaston

33) Nathan Lyon reached 350 test match wickets by dismissing who?
Ben Stokes – 2nd innings at Edgbaston

34) Nathan Lyon moved above Dennis Lillee into 3rd place on the all-time list of Australian wicket-takers by dismissing who?
Joe Root – 2nd innings at Headingley

35) The 2019 series was the first Ashes series in which players had their names and squad numbers on the back of their shirts – can you name the following players from their squad number?
England:
66 (Joe Root)
22 (Jofra Archer)
9 (James Anderson)

Australia:
1 (Usman Khawaja)
31 (David Warner)
49 (Steve Smith)

36) Which two Sky Sports commentators, both former England captains, made their final appearances for the broadcaster in the series?
Ian Botham and David Gower

37) How many hundreds did Steve Smith Score in the series?
3

38) How many times did Stuart Broad dismiss David Warner?
7

39) Who bowled the first ball of the series?
James Anderson

40) Who took the first wicket in the series?
Stuart Broad – dismissing David Warner

41) How many overs did Jimmy Anderson bowl in the series?
4

42) Jofra Archer made his test match debut at Lord's, who did he dismiss for his first test match wicket?
Cameron Bancroft

43) Who became the first ever concussion substitute in a test match during the second test?
Marnus Labuschagne

44) Nathan Lyon missed a clear chance to win the third test with a run out, but which batsman was he attempting to dismiss?
Jack Leach

45) Which umpire incorrectly gave Ben Stokes not out when England required just 2 runs for victory at Headingley?
Joel Wilson

46) Who claimed their only wicket of the series to dismiss Jack Leach in the closing stages of the fourth test as Australia neared victory?
Marnus Labuschagne

47) Who was England's last man out as Australia retained the Ashes?
Craig Overton

48) Who bowled the last ball of the series?
Jack Leach – dismissing Josh Hazlewood

Answers – Decade Records

1) Who made the most appearances for Australia across the decade?
Steve Smith - 27

2) Who made the most appearances for England across the decade?
Stuart Broad - 27

3) Who made the most appearances for either side as captain across the decade?
Michael Clarke – 16

4) Who scored the most runs for Australia across the decade?
Steve Smith – 2800

5) Who scored the most runs for England across the decade?
Alastair Cook - 1995

6) Who took the most wickets for Australia across the decade?
Nathan Lyon - 85

7) Who took the most wickets for England across the decade?
   Stuart Broad – 100

8) How many Ashes hundreds did Alastair Cook score in England?
   0

9) At the end of the 2015 series, how many Ashes series had Ian Bell won with England in his career?
   5

10) What was total score in matches between the sides across the decade?
    England 11-14 Australia

Printed in Great Britain
by Amazon